B.H. Barry Fights for Shakespeare

B.H. Barry Fights for Shakespeare

Book One, Romeo and Juliet

B.H. Barry

ISBN 978-0-557-27704-9

Contents

Introduction

O n the surface, the job of fight directing would seem to be a small part of any production and probably in the minds of many producers, the area on which the smallest amount of the budget should be spent. It is true that the amount of stage time for a fight is minimal compared with the rest of the play but a badly executed fight can destroy a great theatrical moment in a second. Even a simple action like a slap across the face, if not executed effectively, can destroy the audience's suspension of disbelief.

From the "Bardometer Blog" on a fight for Othello that I did in Seattle in June 2009

"The fight scenes were well choreographed and had an element of danger often lacking in this safety-first, block before the blow has even started era of stage combat. (This is the first time I've heard an audience member scream during a fight scene.)

It seems as if this critic had got used to being disappointed by stage combat. What a shame to have created a wonderfully acted play only to have the evening destroyed by the fights. I might add that a badly choreographed fight can also destroy an actor just as quickly.

My job is comparable to that of a magician. I create illusions that are believable, or rather, I show actors how to create these illusions and how to perform them safely.

This booklet has been written in the hope that with the right information and through quality, caring and integrity, wonderful fight scenes will be staged and enhance any production of Romeo and Juliet.

Chapter 1

Beginnings

L et me start by explaining that I did not choose the profession of Fight Director because when I started staging fights back in the 60's, the job of Fight Director did not exist.

Paddy Crean and Barry Jackson were the only people I knew who had anything to do with fights in the theatre. Paddy was an expert fight arranger who was Errol Flynn's stunt double in those wonderful swashbuckling movies, "The Master of Ballantrae" and "The Sword of Sherwood Forest." He was my fencing teacher in the fifties, a master of panache, or as he would say, ZAAA!

He could charm the pants off anyone. Paddy was six feet tall with a full face, a wide mouth sporting above it a pencil thin mustache and spectacular blue eyes, mischievous and wonderfully innocent. He oozed charm and charisma. I have been out to dinner with Paddy when he was in his seventies and waitresses would literally fall in love with him on the spot. He could immortalize a girl's left eyebrow and get away with it. As the waitress arrived at the table he would look at her in awe and as if he had never said it before he would croon,"Isn't she absolutely beautiful B H?" then he would add mischievously

"You are my dear, absolutely beautiful,"and she would go weak in the knees.

As an incurable romantic his fights always had that sense of romantic panache. In 1962 he moved to Canada to work at the Stratford Theatre Festival taking with him his system for using the sword on stage based on the saber parries.

My friendship with Paddy lasted over 30 years. The last time I saw him was in Stratford in Canada. I had been offered a season with The Stratford Festival, Midsummers Nights Dream, Henry IV and Romeo and Juliet. I called Paddy and asked his permission to accept the job. After all he had been their Fight Director for a long time and I had to be sure that I wasn't taking his position. He was, as always, gracious. "Please take the job dear boy," he said," it will be lovely to see you." He saw my fights and I think he enjoyed them, I could see in his eyes that look of pride in what I had achieved. I had taken what he had taught me and had moved stage fights forward into the new genre of realism. Dear, dear Paddy Some people just should not be allowed to die.

Paddy Crean and me at the Stratford Festival Theatre

My other combat teacher at Drama School was Barry Jackson who specialized in unarmed combat, he was a compact man, with close cropped hair. He was solid and self contained and seemingly introverted, but as often is the case with introverted personalities, they are sometimes great actors and he was. As a fight arranger he was known as Jack Barry and he had an enormous effect on my career. Barry was a fight coordinator for theatre and for TV and handed me my first television job.

Barry Jackson

He had decided that he no longer wanted to teach or create fights so he passed his job offers of work onto me. By doing this he jump started my career..

I haven't seen him in years but I did glimpse him on a commercial about a pill to slow down Alzheimer's Disease the other day, and he does not look any older than he did when I first met him. He has a black belt in Aikido, a Japanese martial art. He studied it well before the martial arts became fashionable in England. His unarmed techniques, many of which I use today, were inventive and realistic. I was so lucky to have had these great teachers in my life and to have studied with them when they were in their prime. Not only am I proud they were my mentors but also that they were my friends. It would be remiss of me not to mention my longtime friend William Hobbs. Many an hour we spent together trading ideas on stage fighting. We both taught at

The Central School Of Speech and Drama and on Saturday mornings after class we would meet in the local pub and with some enthusiastic students we would discuss fights we had seen. When Bill was asked to Fight Direct Roman Polanski's movie of Shakespeare's "Macbeth" he invited me to join him. Bill's approach to blade work and mine to unarmed combat, when combined, made those film fights look very different from anything that had been seen before.

Chapter 2

A different approach.

This book is designed to help actors, directors, fight directors and designers to create fights and action for Shakespeare's plays primarily in the theater although the same premises can be used for other mediums.

These are my thoughts and only mine, on creating the fights for Romeo and Juliet for the stage, with the notion that it might help, you, the reader, understand the fights in the play and for you to observe my process in their creation.

I will not be teaching you how to use a sword as there a million different techniques for theatrical swordplay being taught at the moment and I don't wish to confuse the issue. There are also many variations of period rapier and dagger play on the internet and there are many books written about this subject, so I will leave this area alone at the moment.

It is possible to create a fight with one blow as long as the intention of the blow, character and story are maintained. If you are a Fight Director this book will help you to coordinate the ideas of the director, the actor, costume, lighting and sound designers into a sequence of fight scenes that will enhance the characters and the play. If you are not a Fight Director maybe I can answer some of your questions on how to watch, be in, or observe the fights in the exciting story of Romeo and Juliet.

Chapter 3

Recent History

U ntil the 1960's, fights in England were staged pretty much in the same way they had always been; occasionally a person who knew about fights was brought in, as a "fight arranger", but usually it was the actors who organized the fights. The term and the position of "Fight Director" in the theater was only created and accepted in the early sixties.

In Shakespeare's day I can only guess how they put the fights together. Maybe, because swords were used in every day life, the actors would have easily been able to invent sequences on the spot. This is all conjecture, but maybe the lines, "Have at you now," were an indication that the actor was going to attack. "I am dead", could also have been a signal to stop fighting. We will never know, but like most of the myths that surround Shakespeare, his life and his authorship, why not?

In the Victorian period when actors toured their performances, the lead actor often would only have had one day to rehearse with the new company, so sequences of swordplay were developed and repeated. The sequences were given names to differentiate them, such as the "Birmingham Eight, the "Sheffield Ten," and the "Aberdeen Kill." I am making all these titles up, as the real sequences and the names have been lost to antiquity.   When rehearsals started for say, a production of Romeo and Juliet, the two actors in the fight would meet and the lead actor would map out the fight. A conversation might have gone on like this.

Romeo "How do we start?"

Tybalt "Birmingham eight up the stairs"

Romeo "Then?"

Tybalt would then lay out the whole fight using the sequence titles.

During the performance the next day, had you been near enough, to have heard the conversation onstage, you may have heard this…

ROMEO

This shall determine that.

Actor Playing Tybalt (whispers): Birmingham Eight up the

steps.

Then the two actors fight, fight, fight, doing the Birmingham Eight up the steps.

Actor Playing Romeo (whispers) Now what?

Actor Playing Tybalt You do the Sheffield Ten down the

ramp at me!

Then the two actors fight, fight, fight, with Romeo doing the Sheffield Ten down the ramp.

Actor Playing: Tybalt: You kill me with the Aberdeen kill.

Fight executed Tybalt is dead and on with the play.

I remember classes where Paddy would say, "This is the drunken sequence" and would perform a set piece of choreography. If you look at the old films of Douglas Fairbanks both (senior or junior) and those of Errol Flynn, you will notice, in the fights, set sequences of just banging swords together. The ducking the sword, the jumping over the blade, the corps-a corps, the candle chopping and the sword death under the arm, are all part of the very exciting and fun genre.

When I came on the scene that is was what we did, bang swords together. Furthering the character or the story was very much on the back burner. The fight was always considered an event outside the play, a sideshow. The more thrilling the fight the better it was deemed to be. As Paddy would say "remember the ladies in the front row."

Picture the duels in the old films of the 1930s and 40s, like The Three Musketeers or any of the swashbucklers with Errol Flynn. The format remained constant for the story of the fight. The good guy would be in jeopardy at the start of the fight, then he would have to fight back against the bad guy then, against all odds he would win, or some other familiar sequences. The actors would perform their flashy duels and when the fight was over, the dialogue would resume. These fights could be very exciting, but the main purpose of the fight was to show off your stuff and to a celebrate right over wrong.

Now cut to the 1960's. What had been good enough for the classics and film wasn't going to work in the new theatre of naturalism, In fact it wasn't going to work for the classics, either…

In England, in the 60's, a small group of fight choreographers was teaching and working in London. We banded together and called ourselves "Fight Directors." We formed "The British Society of Fight Directors." Our mandate was to share knowledge of stage fighting, create safety rules and to improve the quality of fights in the theatre.

We were being asked to create scenes for the various productions and not just to show someone how to use a sword or throw a punch.

Chapter 4

The Fight Director

M y definition of a Fight Director is this: a person who has a
knowledge of the theatrical techniques of both armed and
unarmed fighting. A person who can train *any* actor to perform a
fight safely and effectively, and, most importantly, a person who
is able to *direct the scenes.* This does not just mean teaching or
choreographing, but possessing the skill which enables the fight
to match and enhance the Director's ideas. Because there are
many different kinds of directors, the fight director must be able
to adapt his work to match seamlessly with the style of the
director's concept of the production. He must be able to adjust
his thinking when talking to the actors so they are not getting
"double signals" about their characters.

When creating a fight I have to take over the scene from
where the talking finishes, to where the first blow is delivered
and then to the end of the altercation and to create it in the same
style as the director.

When a fight director is putting together a fight, he must put
the actor (or his character) into a dangerous situation. Therefore,
he must know how to remove those dangers and be able to

produce a safe and theatrically "dangerous looking" fight. He must advocate, always, for the actor's safety.

Fight Directing is not a job to be taken lightly.

"We are doing a production of Shakespeare's Romeo and Juliet. Are you free and would you like to work on it?" Usually it is a company manager on the phone checking on my availability. Whenever I hear "Shakespeare" my heart leaps. There is no other playwright who can excite me as much as he does. My love affair with Mr. Shakespeare spans 50 years. I have choreographed 27 of the cannon and Romeo and Juliet 53 times. Working on his magnificent plays has enriched both my heart and my bank account. Each production has been different and each and every actor playing Romeo has had a new take on the role. I believe that Shakespeare's longevity in the theater lies in his ability to contact us all on a basic level. He is able to connect to all who can, or have, felt emotion. His plays are explorations into the human condition. Some of his plots are a little suspect but his understanding of what it is to feel is second to none. Pride, love, jealousy, greed, anger-he doesn't miss a trick. He has given me the opportunity to explore, through movement and action, those emotions that exist in all of us.

Chapter 5

The play

I asked a director friend of mine to give me advice on how to direct a Shakespearean play. He replied "First look at the title of the play and that is probably what the play is about." For example Romeo and Juliet is about those two characters and not about Friar Lawrence. The characters names also give us an insight into their function in the play.

Romeo	**Romantic**
Juliet	**Little jewel**
Mercutio	**Mercurial**
Benvolio	**Benevolent**
Tybalt	**The cat (* from the folk tale of "Reynard the Fox" in which the cat is calledTibert).**

Furthermore, he went on, we must ask ourselves, "What human condition is this play exploring?" Anger Pride, love, etc. That will help you to form the emotional structure of the scenes. After that.....

" CAST WELL."

What we identify in his plays is the human condition. I believe that this is the only truth that everyone can, without exception, always agree on.

Chapter 6

General Rules of Truth and Reality

T he truth, or should I say a theatrical version of the truth, is something that we all juggle with in a rehearsal for a play. An actor may claim, "My character would not say that" or " this does not make any sense." These discussions can last quite a while, but most often we will, invariably, settle for what is "dramatic."

The Soap Opera Rule

On the soap opera,"All my Children," for which I served as stunt coordinator, one punch is just an opener for more conversation. In the real world one punch if landed correctly, would do the job of rendering the recipient unconscious, but not on a "Soap"!

This is typical of the dialogue and the action used in Soaps.

BILL

Punches Will in the face.

Why did you insult my girlfriend?

WILL

Getting up and rubbing his chin.

I didn't say anything to her.

On TV soaps we accept "separate reality" it is part of its world so we go along with it.

So it is with theatre. We make the rules. Providing we are consistent, the audience will usually go along with us.

The Walt Disney concept of reality;

Gravity does not exist until the character recognizes that it exists. They will not fall until they realize that there is nothing beneath their feet and/or paws, or until he/she or it, looks down.

Another Realism Rule

Realism can bite you in the butt as a fight director when the audience becomes more fearful for the actor and not for the character. e.g.

In John Simon's review of The Late Henry Moss he writes I quote,

"Arliss Howard is a bit too slight to make a suitable adversary as Earl. My heart went out to him during a brutal fight, dazzlingly devised by B. H. Barry, in which Ray wipes up the floor with him, and then supererogatory makes him wipe the same floor with a rag."

End quote.

The fight was too real. We felt compassion for the actor and not for the character. The fight it also drew attention to itself.

If I have really directed a fight well, you should not be able to tell where the director left off and I began. The play, in question was, a new Sam Shepherd piece, "The Late Henry Moss" starring Ethan Hawke, a wonderful film and stage actor. It was the other actor, Arliss Howard who complained that he hated fights on stage because they did not look real. In defense of this actor he did put his heart and soul into the task but we finished up with more sympathy for him than for the character.

We can make believe anything on stage, from a tempest to a dark night where ghosts abound. In the theatre we are not restricted by reality. We try to make the stories we tell resonate in the minds of the audience and so we use different ploys to create this resonance.

The dialect that was spoken in the 16th century is almost indecipherable to the modern ear. It could be argued that this is how the works of Shakespeare should be performed-using that dialect so as to be historically true to the text. Because we need to understand the words we have updated the pronunciation. I am sure that when I choreograph a Shakespearean fight I am not being authentic. My mission is to create a fight that fits the human condition within the play and satisfies both the characters and the story.

There are many experts on period fencing who know the classic moves and they have studied Fabris, Saviolo, DiGrassi, Silver and many other sword masters at length and know all the correct positions of the hands and feet when executing a thrust or a parry. I will freely admit that although I am fascinated by the historical treatises on weapons and of the vocal dialects of the period, this information takes a back seat to the dramatic content of the scene. My exception to this statement would be in film where one can shoot and edit in detail and use the medium to tell the story. In theater where we are creating our own kind of detail, storytelling is my major pursuit.

The average audience usually has little or no knowledge of the intricacies of fencing but they do have an awareness of right and wrong and of cheating and fair play.

I will often bring in drawings of fencing positions used in the period to establish a frame of reference, but to sacrifice the human condition to the point of realism is unjust and self serving. A fight in a play on stage should, like the dialogue, be more theatrical than in real life, it should convey a heightened sense of reality. The characters use specific dialogue to express their thoughts to each other and to the audience. So should it be with the action in a fight. Slaps and punches should be bigger and with more sound, also sequences with weapons should indicate character and story.

In a fight scene, most of the audience will not know the difference between demi-volte and a passado. Do we really want the audience to say? "that was well executed demi-volte!" or would we rather have the reaction? "My God! at that moment I thought Romeo was going to die." There is an argument to have both, but my fights are usually about survival and when push comes to shove, historically, historical truth rushes for the exit. Drama triumphs.

Obviously some scenes in Shakespeare require a degree of authenticity, like using a sword and not an AK 47, if the play is set in the 16th century, but to become a slave of what is historically true and real, seems to me, redundant. We are not creating a museum piece. Having written this I do realize that it is true an audience can be wowed by authenticity. I have seen costumes on stage and in movies that have taken my breath away and sets that are magnificent and in the right circumstances are valid and do add a lot to the setting of the period in the play.

A wonderful designer Abdul Farrar said to me once, that two elements were important to him in the theater,"if you have spent money on the set it should look as you have spent money and furthermore if you have rehearsed the play it should look as if you had rehearsed the play. Mind you," he added," "if it looks as if you have spent money but didn't and if it looked as if you had rehearsed but hadn't, that was OK too." The maxim "less is more" is to be paid attention too. I will also add to the phrase. "Unless more becomes necessary."

This probably a good time to look at the other departments of the production and see how they influence the fights.

Chapter 7

Set Designers

I try to incorporate the set in my fights. Occasionally reality rears its head and I am confronted with major set pieces. Stairs, balconies, bars, doors, washing.

In one production of Romeo and Juliet I was confronted with washing on the stage; not just one line but a whole bunch configured in the shape of a Z. I had been working with the director on the big mob fight at the beginning of Act 1. It was rather involved and I had several actors doing choreographed fighting moves with buckets, poles, swords and various other marketplace gear. We had been rehearsing the fight scene in London and were going to Stratford upon Avon to perform it at the Royal Shakespeare Company Theater there. I had been informed there would be an empty stage but on arriving in the theater, there on stage, was all this **washing**."What's all this?" I asked the director who was showing no signs of surprise at the spectacle. "Oh" he said "I thought it would be effective if the scene was set in a place where they dyed clothes" hence the **WASHING**. There was no place to fight without getting tangled in the clothes. So I used what was there .....

ABRAHAM

You lie

SAMPSON

Draw if you be men. Gregory, remember thy .....washing

blow.

(Maybe that's where the director got the idea.)
Then they all pulled down the washing.
A friend of mine and I gave awards to inanimate objects for their contribution to the arts.
Categories included.
Best use of an actor by a costume.
Best use of an actor by an enforced piece of blocking.
Best use on an actor by a prop.
Best use of an actor by a beard, facial hair and or wig.
Best use of an actor by a set. WASHING would have won this category .All the above categories should answer to two masters in a play. Do they enhance the story or the characters? The same rule goes for a fight.

Chapter 8

Costume Designer

T he stage can be a dangerous place.
Loose shirt ties, slippery shoes and too tight trousers. I never have a problem with hats, unless it is an ill fitting helmet. I have seen an actor turn right and his helmet not move, leaving him looking through the right ear hole. All head apparel must be well fitted. A hat can really help to define a character but it can also be dangerous. Like a mustache or a beard a hat needs to be nailed down. A hat should be fixed firmly to the actor (maybe with a staple gun.) I jest! That would ruin the hat! The shirt sleeves in this period were closed together using ties. The trouble that these can cause is endless. The ties, as if by magic, will entangle the quillions, (cross pieces on a sword), quicker than you can say thrust, not allowing the sword to move, leaving the actor fighting with his shirt while the other actor looks on. The costumes could be authentic, but using zippers, Velcro and buttons are useful to the actor and great aids for quick changes.

Shoes can be lethal, especially if they have shiny soles, or someone has decided to use real flowers on stage. Wedding scene: in one performance, the director decided to have real flowers strewn before the couple as they leave the chapel after their marriage. (A contender for the prize. **Best use of an actor by a prop.**) One of the first rules of theatre..stay away from liquids on stage. Flowers become liquid when you step on them as Bernard Lloyd (Mercutio) found out during the fight. Bernard almost skated off the stage. Adding to the dilemma, the stage was covered by a metal grating. Which brings us to the next costume check. Make sure you can move in your trousers so that when you go into a big lunge they don't split. Real flowers and tight trousers and a metal stage are not a good combination. That night Bernard gave his all. Every article of clothing can prove to be a menace so think ahead. Costumes should be loose enough to allow movement. Make sure you can lift your hands above your head. If there is a sword blow to the head and you cannot lift your sword above your head to defend yourself, then you are in deep doodoo.

At the costume fitting, speak up. It is better to do the alterations early on than wait for the first tech.

Chapter 9

Lighting and sound

Rule one and two.

Make sure that you can see what you are doing.

Any light set to project its beam from lower than 45 degrees will hit the actors in the eyes, making it hard for them to see the blades.

Beware shin-busters.

Lights from the floor shining upwards. This effect though dramatic, totally blinds the actors.

A fight will look its best if the combatants move in and out of light. The effect will add to the drama and make the blades seem to travel faster.

Sound.

Music that runs through a play can help make the links between scenes, set up mood or enhance a dramatic moment. The background music should support the mood of the fight rather than dictate the rhythm.

Chapter 10

Reality can be hazardous to your health.

Any liquid will, sure enough, migrate to the stage deck, causing the actor to slip. Also dangerous are suits of armor made in period that are too heavy for the actor to move in as with swords that are authentic but unwieldy for the actor, the list is endless of how realism can be taken to far. Blood if used correctly can bring cries of horror from the audience but too much blood can get a big laugh.

Making weapons out of the correct period metal and balancing them to cause the most damage could be argued for in war, but on stage and with the average actor, a well balanced and light sword can be used with much more excitement and with a higher degree of safety. Making a Broadsword out of high grade aluminum is something I would strongly recommend. Usually the actor has to perform eight times a week, which means he has to perform two shows on one day. Making the sword light will be another factor in making the fight safer and more effective.

Chapter 11

On the subject of weapons.

I have been working with the same armorer for close to 50 years. He has the perfect name for a maker of theatrical swords, **Alan Meek.** His swords have been seen in many motion pictures, operas, ballets and TV both here in America and across Europe. He is a true artisan. His weapons are beautiful to look at and are perfect for any actor. They are wonderfully balanced and seem to stand up to abuse.

Placing a dangerous and unbalanced weapon in the hands of an actor can end in a real tragedy.

To check the balance of a sword.

The ideal weapon should feel comfortable when you pick it up. You should experience its weight in your hand and not in the blade. If you feel that the blade is tipping you forward it will mean that you have less control when you fight with it. A great sword is like a great costume-it should help the actor rather than hindering him or her.

The fights in Romeo and Juliet are a fight director's dream. They are fought by young actors and they use, if we stay in period and true to the text, rapier and dagger.

Choice Of Weapons

Let's go to a choice of weapons for the play. I believe from the text that the young nobles are wearing rapier and dagger. The servants could be holding anything, from daggers to quarter staffs. There are several references to weapons.

Sampson and Gregory enter with swords and Bucklers. A buckler is a small round shield carried on the waist. It was used as a form of defense in that period.

Sword & buckler performers at play from the late 1300s.

SAMPSON

My naked weapon is out; quarrel and I will back thee.

BENVOLIO

Put up your swords. (He could change the line to "staves")

TYBALT

What, art thou drawn among these heartless hinds?

(Notice..Benvolio has a sword)

Turn thee, Benvolio, look upon thy death

BENVOLIO

I do but keep the peace: put up thy sword,

(Notice....Tybalt also must have sword.)

Or manage it to part these men with me.

TYBALT

What, drawn, and talk of peace! I hate the word,

As I hate hell, all Montagues, and thee:

Have at thee, coward!

They fight.

**A partisan and bills, a spear like weapons, would have been used
by the guards**

*Enter, several of both houses, who join the fray; then enter
Citizens, with clubs* (Notice. clubs)

FIRST CITZEN

Clubs, bills, and partisans!

(Is this a call for help?)

strike! beat them down!

Down with the Capulets! down with the Montagues!

Enter CAPULET in his gown, and LADY CAPULET

CAPULET

What noise is this? Give me my long sword, ho!

(Notice Long Sword)

LADY CAPULET

A crutch, a crutch! why call you for a sword?

CAPULET

My sword, I say! Old Montague is come, And flourishes his blade in spite of me.

So if we do this play in the correct period we need;
2 Rapiers swords first fight.
Sword for Mercutio (Romeo will use this sword to kill Tybalt)
Sword for Paris
(2 Daggers)
2 other servant type weapons
Clubs bills partisans (Partisans and bills are kinds of spears
or pikes)
Various market type props
2 long swords
and possibly swords for the guards.
A dagger for Romeo

Chapter 12

Style of Fighting

T here are indications in the script as to the form of rapier and dagger play of the period, and especially about Tybalt's style which need to be paid attention to.

MERCUTIO

More than prince of cats, I can tell you. O, he is

the courageous captain of compliments. He fights as

you sing prick-song, keeps time, distance, and

proportion; a reference to Tybalt's preciseness ...

rests me his minim rest, one, two, and the third in your

bosom:

This refers to a compound attack, pretending to attack one place causing the defender to open up another target, then instantly attacking that target to cause confusion and finally landing the blow in an unprotected area. It seems to me that this is the use of the point rather than the cutting edge although it can be done with either.

the very butcher of a silk button, a duellist, a duellist; a

gentleman of the very first house, of the first and second

cause:

ah, the immortal passado! A forward thrust
the punto reverso! A backward thrust, the point in reverse
the hai! A fleche attack, leaping forward.

All these comments by Mercutio could allude to a new style of fighting with sword and dagger. It seems that the old practice with rapier and dagger was conducted like this-a circle was drawn on the ground and the fighters would stand opposite each other. If fighter A took a step to the right then fighter B would to move to his right, each now occupying the next quadrant of the circle on their right. Blows were delivered one at a time.

Capo Fero

Shadows seem to indicate different positions of on-guard. The figure on the left has turned sideways, very modern!

the immortal passado! the punto reverso! the hai!

These phrases, from what I can gather, refer to movements across the circle rather than to the side. Whatever the explanation about the different styles of rapier play, and I am sure there will be many, what is important, is that Mercutio regards the new style with contempt.

I try to concern myself with the story and the characters and I rely on the acting to give an indication of the style. " He fights by the book of arithmetic." says Mercutio of Tybalt. Armed with this information we could, at the start of the fight, show the differences in their styles. Tybalt could come on-guard using an elaborate stance and Mercutio could make fun of him by exaggeratedly copying Tybalt's action .

MERCUTIO

The pox of such antic, lisping, affecting

fantasticoes; these new tuners of accents! 'By Jesu,

a very good blade! a very tall man! a very good

whore!' Why, is not this a lamentable thing,

grandsire, that we should be thus afflicted with

these strange flies, these fashion-mongers, these

pardonnez-moi's, who stand so much on the new form, that

they cannot sit at ease on the old bench? O, their bones,

their bones!

If we were to take this speech away from the play we would not know that Mercutio and Tybalt use the sword differently. Mercutio is a street fighter, Tybalt is more formal.

Chapter 13

Remove the fight.

A fight in Shakespeare, if removed from the play, leaves a gaping hole in the plot, both emotionally and structurally. He never uses an action sequence gratuitously. There is always a reason for the fight.

Let Us Now Put it all in order.

The play is called Romeo and Juliet so it is probably about Romeo and Juliet. Which of the human conditions does the play mainly deal with? Young love; what it is to be young and in love. What it is to feel love. My own observation: There are two questions that I always ask when talking to the director or to the actors.

1 What would be missing from the play if the fights were removed from the production?

2 What would be missing from the character's performances?

3 How would the elimination of the fight affect the story and the characters?

The answers to these questions should give a clear indication how the fight should be staged.

Chapter 14

The first fight.

There are three fights in R & J, four if you count Mercutio v Tybalt and Romeo v Tybalt as two separate fights. This first fight, in the market Square, appears to be a display of who is "in the right," but on further examination and applying my acid test....

1 "What would be missing from the play if this fight were eliminated?"

...something different appears. We would not see the volatile world of Verona or the deep-seated hatred between the Capulets and the Montagues. True, the argument begins with who is in the right, but it is the feud that we need to know about, the necessary background to the romance between Romeo and Juliet. If there is no feud ...two kids get married, end of play.

The first fight has to show this hatred and it must finish with the Montagues and the Capulets at odds with each other.

A new quarrel started.

PROLOGUE

Two households, both alike in dignity,

In fair Verona, where we lay our scene,

From ancient grudge break to new mutiny,

Where civil blood makes civil hands unclean.

Interestingly it is the servants who start the fight, culminating with the parents going at it. This was a town at peace until this moment. We are privileged to be at the rebirth of this new quarrel.

"From ancient grudge break to new mutiny"

Tybalt is the only character who is given the task of inciting hostility. Whenever he comes on stage there is nothing but trouble. No one else is interested in continuing this "ancient grudge" until this character appears.

ABRAHAM

"Do you bite your thumb at us sir?"

SAMPSON

"No sir! But I do bite my thumb."

GREGORY

Seeing Tybalt.

"Say better here comes my masters kinsman."

Tybalt repeats the hostility during the party, and when the boys are in the market square. Without him we would not have the present threat of death. This not to say that he marches through the play hissing and shouting but he does carry the quarrel with him wherever he goes. We never discover what the original argument was about, but does it matter?

The events
1 Servants enter
They fight
2 Benvolio enters

3 Tybalt enters
They fight
4 The elders enter.
They fight
5 In comes the Prince

These are the facts in all the plays, operas and ballet versions. In opera and in the ballet, the events alter somewhat, but on the whole, stick to Shakespeare's plan.

Let us look at the servant's moment.

The servants seem to be comic characters who are meant to give us a few laughs.

This is a great device on Shakespeare's part, it allows for an emotional progression-laughter to tears.   What a wonderful opportunity for the fight director to explore this journey. As with modern wars it all starts with a single action.   Somebody has to deliver the first blow, fire the first shot, drop the first bomb. That first blow should be momentous.

I was working with Rudolf Nureyev on his R&J and I was choreographing the wally out of the Mercutio v Tybalt fight. In the midst of my creative display of "choreographic genius" he came up to me and said " Don't open all your Christmas presents at once." "What do you mean", I said? He replied, "When I dance a solo, at the beginning of the dance, I open with big Christmas present, then, I dance, bullshit, bullshit, then small Christmas present then, bullshit, bullshit and finally one big CHRISTMAS PRESENT."

"So, don't open all Christmas presents at once.

I think this advice could be used in any creative situation.

Back to the servants' fight.

It is true one could use servant type swords, lightweight broadswords or a simple cross hilt sword, but I like to go for less swordlike weapons to begin the fight with. My particular favorite for this fight is the quarterstaff. The reason-they are more servant like weapons. Benvolio and Tybalt increase the danger by using metal. The quarterstaff looks and feels rustic. It is also showy and a lot of fun.

So stage 1 of the first fight..Quarterstaff with....

Sampson

Gregory

Abraham

Serving man

Information that we glean from the script.

There is a code of behavior, the rules of engagement, if you like, before a fight can begin. Once it is set in motion there is very little that can be done to stop it. The final result of this code is enacted when Romeo has to kill Tybalt. Tybalt has killed Mercutio and according to the code, Romeo must kill Tybalt. This is set up in the first fight when Tybalt calls Benvolio a coward.

LADY CAPULET

I beg for justice, which thou, prince, must give;

Romeo slew Tybalt, Romeo must not live.

PRINCE

Romeo slew him, he slew Mercutio;

Who now the price of his dear blood doth owe?

In some countries, this code exists in a form which transcends common sense. An eye for an eye, a tooth for a tooth, a never ending cycle of violence. The right to exact revenge. The right to defend one's honor to the death is one thing, but, the misery that is caused by revenge, is another element of the human condition that this play addresses.

SAMPSON

Is the law on our side if I say ay?"

I am not going to have an opinion here, all I know is I am going to, *"hold the mirror up to nature."*

The dialogue leads us through the preliminaries till we get to the fight.

SAMPSON

Draw if you be men. Gregory remember thy washing blow."

This line could be interpreted as a linear statement, advice to Gregory or ... to make it funny, Sampson offers the challenge" *Draw if you be men."* then makes Gregory fight by handing the staff to him and pushing him forward saying the line. *Gregory remember thy washing blow."*

So we start the fight with a laugh, which escalates into something much bigger.

Benvolio will be forced to fight to save face. This foreshadows the fights to come. Next Mercutio will be forced to save Romeo's face, followed by Tybalt and finally Romeo.

All of them are prompted into action to save face.

Stage 2 of fight
Enter BENVOLIO (in such a way that he doesn't see Tybalt)

BENVOLIO

Part, fools!

Put up your swords; you know not what you do.

Beats down their swords/staves
Enter Tybalt

TYBALT

What, art thou drawn among these heartless hinds?

Turn thee, Benvolio, look upon thy death.

BENVOLIO

I do but keep the peace: put up thy sword,

Or manage it to part these men with me.

TYBALT

What, drawn, and talk of peace! I hate the word,

As I hate hell, all Montagues, and thee:

At this point I usually have Benvolio choose to leave. He almost makes it when Tybalt calls after him.

Have at thee, coward!

Benvolio's return to fight will heighten the fact that he has to fight Tybalt to save his honor.

Notice the colon after thee and the comma after thee,[pause]

Coward!

Benvolio is forced into action.

I wonder how many altercations have been set into motion after the use of that word, coward?

The fight is now about to escalate, turning from a minor disturbance into a fully fledged fight, with death as a possible outcome. There is the opportunity for both Benvolio and Tybalt to demonstrate to the audience something about their characters, during this exchange of blows. You might think of the characters as archetypes, thus:

Tybalt the expert sword fighter.

Benvolio the novice.

Tybalt the bully.

Benvolio the victim.

Benvolio the short tempered.

Tybalt the crafty.

Any or all of these facets of their characters can be added to the fight.

I believe this fight has been put there to show Tybalt's expertise and the ever-present danger of his presence. He is now a threat to peace and a physically dangerous presence in the play.

I have found that by taking Tybalt and Benvolio off-stage with their fight we are able to focus more on the leaders of the two houses. To jump ahead-I have Tybalt chase Benvolio off and when they return Benvolio is chasing Tybalt. This is a great opportunity to create a moment. If.... The Prince is already onstage when an enraged Benvolio runs on, he is the only one with a sword in his hands and the only one left fighting. Oh! The irony! The one who tried to make peace is the one who is seen fighting.

So the sequence runs like this;

Servants fight.

Tybalt and Benvolio fight and run off.

Capulet and Montague have at each other

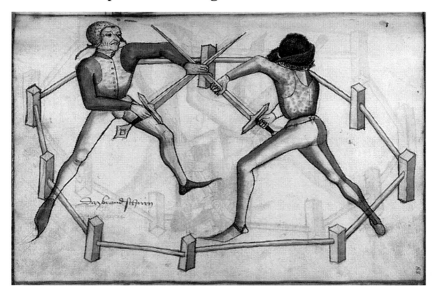

Everyone fights…

ATTACK ON A POTATO STORE.

In come the guards.

Fight between the Rioters in Kensington.

Then in comes the Prince

PRINCE

Rebellious subjects-enemies to peace,

Profaners of this neighbour-stained steel;-

Will they not hear?................What ho! you men..........

Guards break up fight. Fight stops.
In comes Tybalt chased by Benvolio who doesn't see the Prince.
Benvolio caught "with his trousers down." Embarrassed.

PRINCE

On pain of torture, from those bloody hands

Throw your mistempered weapons to the ground,.....

So ends the first fight.

Chapter 15

Overall look at the second and third fights.

I always think of these fights as the fulcrum on which the play exists, the balance between the first and second parts of Romeo and Juliet. Without these fights we would not have a second act. When Tybalt dies and Romeo is banished the world of the play changes. Unlike many Shakespeare's fights, these happen right in the middle of the play propelling the separation between Romeo and Juliet. The usual finish to the first act is where Romeo is banished by the Prince. I think I prefer opening the second act with the market square scene and the fights. Although it makes the second act longer, I believe it enables us and the actor playing Romeo to make a better emotional journey. Closing the first act with the duels although climatic, takes all the joy out of Mudville. Mercutio is dead, no more yuks, all that's left are tears. By having the fights open the second act, Mercutio is alive and there are still some yuks to come before it all goes pear shaped. We have a beautiful wedding and what a great ending to the first act. (one could use real flowers as long as they are cleared during the interval).

Laughter before tears.

Every time I have worked on this piece I've found that Mercutio has always been the most popular character with audiences and his death has been the most tragic. Killing a clown is not good. His sharp wit, and his sexual innuendoes, have always made audiences love him, (especially teenagers) and for Shakespeare to kill him off so early is a very bold choice. Then again, If you consider the only other character to sacrifice, it would have to be Benvolio, then one realizes that it has to be Mercutio who has to die. Killing Benvolio would be sad but to kill Mercutio is tragic. Mercutio represents Romeo's past life, a teenager with no responsibilities. Killing Mercutio propels Romeo into adulthood, and causes Romeo's loss of innocence.

ROMEO

I am fortunes fool!

Mercutio is neither a Capulet nor a Montague. He is the Prince's kinsman so that somehow allows the Prince to show a glimmer of mercy in judging Romeo for the death of Tybalt.

PRINCE

Not death but banishment.

Chapter 16

The Mercutio V. Tybalt fight.

I f we were to remove these fights from the play the only barrier to Romeo and Juliet living out their lives together, would be their parents consent. The fights have to be there to create a larger problem for the lovers. The result of these fights has to end with Romeo's banishment.

What human condition are we exploring here? Teenage passion. The all consuming teenage need to be in the right. The willingness to confront death, to prove yourself. The need to feel the danger of the moment and not know the outcome. Finally the close relationship between love, hate and sacrifice.

We, the audience, observe the lack of accountability and we should want to intervene.

ROMEO

Away to heaven, respective lenity,

And fire-eyed fury be my conduct now!

The scene opens with references to how hot it is and how the heat can effect tempers.

BENVOLIO

I pray thee, good Mercutio, let's retire:

The day is hot, the Capulets abroad,

And, if we meet, we shall not scape a brawl;

For now, these hot days, is the mad blood stirring.

Romeo has been sent an insulting letter and Mercutio is out to take revenge on Romeo's behalf. Benvolio ever the peace maker, is trying to calm the situation. Tybalt arrives and Mercutio goes after him. Tybalt accuses Mercutio of **consorting** with Romeo. There are two possibilities here for interpretation.

1 Pacifying Mercutio by saying;

Consort;
Habitually associate with (someone), typically with the disapproval of others: you chose to consort with the enemy.
Or
2 Insulting Mercutio
Consort;
A wife, husband, or companion, in particular the spouse of a reigning monarch.
A rather childish way of insulting someone, suggesting they are in a sexual relationship! This is possibly the first documented homophobic remark ever made on the stage!

To have the implication of "consorts with" seems to be much more of an insult and after all there is no love lost between Tybalt and Mercutio. If we use the first definition it would suggest that Tybalt didn't want to fight Mercutio and that he was saying my fight is not with you. If that were the case Mercutio's reply "does thou make us minstrels" takes on another meaning i.e.. Mercutio is looking for a reason to kick Tybalt's butt. Using the second definition provokes Mercutio and forces him into action.

Just as they are about to go at it, in comes Romeo. He could have taken a different way home but fate would not have it so. Tybalt insults Romeo.

1973 RST:

Timothy Dalton (Romeo),

Estelle Kohler (Juliet),

Bernard Lloyd (Mercutio),

David Suchet (Tybalt),

PeterMachin (Benvolio),

David Suchet, who plays Poiret in the B.B.C. series of the same name, was playing Tybalt. David had been a student of mine at The London Academy of Music and Dramatic Art, and a great stage fighter. We were looking for a way to say more about his character when we came up with the revolutionary idea,-what if Tybalt had been lying about his ability to fight, emulating the popular Karate nut who knew all the moves but couldn't fight, and that he, Tybalt was in fact a devout coward? How did we support this idea? In the first scene of the play Tybalt, knowing that Benvolio was an even worse fighter than he was, felt he could pick on him.

As far as Tybalt challenging Romeo: If he knows that Romeo is seeing Juliet romantically he can safely assume Romeo will do nothing to upset her by fighting him, she is his cousin after all. So he can challenge Romeo without fear that Romeo will fight. Also the Prince had banned fighting, so Tybalt thinks Mercutio will not take up arms and that he is home free. I know that these reasons are all "back story" but they can add a wonderful IF to the scene. So-

IF-Benvolio didn't know that Tybalt was a coward.
IF - Mercutio didn't care that Tybalt was a coward.
IF Romeo did care.

Each one now has his own, different, reason for dealing with the situation on hand. " ***The bigger the problem, the better the answer.*** " I love these problems and I know that actors do too.

Fate has it that Romeo, on the way home from marrying Juliet bumps into the group.

Now Tybalt challenges Romeo and Romeo refuses to fight to protect his honor.

TYBALT

Romeo, the hate I bear thee can afford

No better term than this,--thou art a villain.

This the challenge and the insult.

 The lie direct.

To understand this statement better we can have a look at one of Shakespeare's other plays. "As you like it." In it Touchstone explains how a quarrel can turn into an insult resulting in a challenge to fight a duel and then how to avoid the duel.

TOUCHSTONE

O sir, we quarrel in print, by the book; as you have

books for good manners: I will name you the degrees.

The first, the Retort Courteous; the second, the

Quip Modest; the third, the Reply Churlish; the

fourth, the Reproof Valiant; the fifth, the

Countercheque Quarrelsome; the sixth, the Lie with

Circumstance; the seventh, the Lie Direct. All

these you may avoid but the Lie Direct;

and you may avoid that too, with an If. I knew when seven

justices could not take up a quarrel, but when the

parties were met themselves, one of them thought but

of an If, as, 'If you said so, then I said so;' and

they shook hands and swore brothers. Your If is the

only peacemaker; much virtue in If.

Obviously Shakespeare was familiar with the rules of dueling and so probably was his audience. It would look from the dialogue that Romeo had successfully escaped the challenge by Tybalt. A clever piece of writing by the Bard.
So Romeo replies,

ROMEO

Tybalt, the reason that I have to love thee

Doth much excuse the appertaining rage

To such a greeting: villain am I none;

Therefore farewell; I see thou know'st me not.(the Reproof

Valiant;)

TYBALT

Boy, this shall not excuse the injuries

That thou hast done me; therefore turn and draw.

(Countercheque Quarrelsome;)

ROMEO

I do protest, I never injured thee,

But love thee better than thou canst devise,

Till thou shalt know the reason of my love:

And so, good Capulet,--which name I tender

As dearly as my own,--be satisfied. (the Retort Courteous;)

Mercutio feels all manner of emotions at this point. He put himself on the line to protect Romeo and Romeo has let him down.

MERCUTIO

O calm, dishonourable, vile submission!

Alla stoccata carries it away. alla stoccata, meaning, with

one thrust he wins.

Draws

Tybalt, you rat-catcher, will you walk? (The lie direct, Tybalt has to fight)

At this point I should explain that David Suchets' Tybalt has been seen strutting around with a henchman who has been carrying five or six swords that Tybalt flourishes at any given opportunity with a degree of ostentation, like those guys who at the drop of a hat go into a Karate sequence.

The point is, we know that Tybalt is a sham. When he gets called out by Mercutio we feel pity for him.

TYBALT

What wouldst thou have with me?

MERCUTIO

Good king of cats, nothing but one of your nine

lives; that I mean to make bold withal, and as you

shall use me hereafter, drybeat the rest of the

eight. Will you pluck your sword out of his pitcher

by the ears? make haste, lest mine be about your

ears ere it be out.

TYBALT

I am for you.

Drawing.

I have always felt the need to illustrate the difference between Mercutio's way of fighting and that of Tybalt's. A modern example would be Karate as opposed to street fighting, the formal meets the informal. Mercutio describes Tybalts way of fighting and his contempt for it .

MERCUTIO

The pox of such antic, lisping, affecting fantasticoes; these new tuners of accents! —'By Jesu, a very good blade! —A very tall man! —A very good whore!'—Why, is not this a lamentable thing, grandsire, that we should be thus afflicted with these strange flies, these fashion-mongers, these pardonnez-mois, who stand so much on the new form that they cannot sit at ease on the old bench? O, their bons, their bons! [bones]

As in most fights, death is an option-Fighting with sharp swords it would seem that death would have been the objective. Theatrically there are many options here.

What IF.
Mercutio wants to force Romeo to fight Tybalt? So he puts himself at risk.

Tybalt wants to get Romeo to fight him and sets about humiliating Mercutio?

Mercutio is going to humiliate Tybalt?

In this production I used the last **IF**

Let us see how by using this **if** we can make the scene more interesting. Romeo tries to stop the "lesson" that Mercutio is going to give Tybalt. Benvolio can't wait to see it happen, so he holds Romeo back. At this point I am trying to make the audience feel that the whole fight is a big joke. The funnier the beginning of the duel is, the more horrific the death will seem. The fight will have many amusing incidents with Mercutio taking increasingly chances with Tybalt. Just as Mercutio delivers the final humiliation, Romeo steps in and stops Mercutio. At that moment Tybalt breaks free of the men who were helping him up and runs Mercutio through, (*Side note, I have played this moment; that seeing Romeo with his back to him. Tybalt decides to run Romeo through but Mercutio sees this, and moves Romeo aside and takes the blow himself.*) You will notice that I have made no mention of what blows to deliver. Sequences are made up within the capabilities of the actors and their demands. It could be decided that only the cutting edge of the sword will be used by Mercutio and the point by Tybalt and then let the fight degenerate into the more lethal point.

Mercutio could, as a street fighter, use kicks and trips and so on.

Have at you now!

David Suchet and Bernard Lloyd

I am fortunes fool!, **Timothy Dalton and David Suchet**

La Jolla Playhouse

1983 Season

Romeo and Juliet

Robert Joy,	*Mercutio*
David Patrick Kelly,	*Tybalt*
Amanda Plummer,	*Juliet*
Vyto Ruginis,	*Benvolio*
John Vickery,	*Romeo*

The big moment in this fight was when David Patrick Kelly, as Tybalt, launched himself at Robert Joy, Mercutio, from a bridge that had been erected on stage. Let me explain.

Heidi Landesman had designed a set that had a bridge that spanned the whole of the stage. Peter Brook would have been proud, for it was on that bridge that actors could fill the empty space, both below and above. This is a signature feature in the sets used by Des MacAnuff. Fair enough....visually this can be splendid, but it does have its drawbacks. Because the top deck has to be supported, the supports can limit the acting area of the space below it, forcing the blocking to be square and flat. I love diagonals on the stage. They give depth to the action and help the dynamic of the space to achieve more than a flat TV look.

The bigger the problem the better the answer.

I have always believed in embracing problems. The best theatrical moments can be born out of dilemmas. Conflict, of one sort or another, is what theater is all about.

So how did I use the bridge?

I like the idea of starting the Mercutio - Tybalt fight with a sense of fun, dangerous fun. These are kids after all, and games of chicken involving danger are meat and potatoes to teens. The thought of death or injury takes second place to ego and derring do. So it is with the human condition. How often does the phrase, "it will all end in tears" prove to be true?

MERCUTIO

O calm, dishonourable, vile submission!

Alla stoccata carries it away.

Draws

Tybalt, you rat-catcher, will you walk?

TYBALT

What wouldst thou have with me?

MERCUTIO

Good king of cats, nothing but one of your nine

lives; that I mean to make bold withal, and as you

shall use me hereafter, drybeat the rest of the

eight. Will you pluck your sword out of his pitcher

by the ears? make haste, lest mine be about your

ears ere it be out.

TYBALT

I am for you.

Drawing his sword

At this point Mercutio, being mercurial, changes the rules to-let's play a game. Having done the fight so often I had always run into the problem of what to do with Romeo while Tybalt and Mercutio were fighting. His lines suggest that he is trying to intervene.

ROMEO

Draw, Benvolio; beat down their weapons.

Gentlemen, for shame, forbear this outrage!

Tybalt, Mercutio, the prince expressly hath

Forbidden bandying in Verona streets:

Hold, Tybalt! good Mercutio!

Does Romeo just stand there and yell? Or does he run around like demented chicken offering advice. Who holds him back, and why? It could be argued that Benvolio does this task because Tybalt came after him in the first scene. I think that it would be in Benvolio's best interest to see Tybalt humiliated. Dramatically how much more interesting would it be to have the fight start innocently and gradually become more violent, causing the already hot Tybalt to lose his temper? What if Mercutio provokes Tybalt orally and then goads him physically? What if the dangerous game gets out of hand? Tybalt has no reason to fight Mercutio. Of course he was insulted "**Rat Catcher**" is not a compliment. Does he strike out of anger? Or is it an accident that he kills Mercutio? Whatever happens, Romeo has to be responsible for Mercutio's death in some way.

MERCUTIO

Why the devil came you between us? I

was hurt under your arm.

ROMEO

I thought all for the best.

So how did I use the bridge?

Mercutio angers Tybalt and makes him chase him. Mercutio dodges Tybalt who finishes up on the bridge completely confused, with a triumphant Mercutio on stage level. Everybody laughs at Tybalt's confusion. Tybalt, without thinking, leaps eight feet from the bridge towards Mercutio and onto the crowd below. It'a a big moment for Tybalt, a surprise moment for Mercutio and a thrilling moment for the audience.

Welcome bridge!

Chapter 17

Many Productions

E xamples of some of the games played, all culminating with Tybalt losing his temper.

1980

Guhrie Minneapolis.

Director	*Ron Daniels*
Romeo	*(Christopher Rich)*
Tybalt	*(Larkin Malloy)*
Mercutio	*(Justin Deas)*

This Romeo and Julliet was set in a futuristic world. We had all-purpose costumes and a shiny blue plastic floor. The use of rapier and dagger was redundant so I had to come up with a weapon or weapons that could fit the style. Based on the statement from the Prince,

PRINCE

If ever you disturb our streets again,

Your lives shall pay the forfeit of the peace.

I thought the weapons might be concealed.   My answer? Riding crops that housed short swords.   I could now use the sheath as a defensive weapon and the blade to attack with.   *To begin with the swords are sheathed and Mercutio and Tybalt tie themselves together with a scarfs held in their left hands.   The "pissing Tybalt off moment."   Mercutio lets go of the scarf and Tybalt falls over.   Tybalt loses his temper, draws a sword from his riding crop and off we go.*
Then there was

1981

Director	**Barry Davis**
Mercutio	**Jack Wetheral**
Romeo	**Tom Hulce**
Benvolio	**Peter Gallagher**
Tybalt	**Gary Sloan**

Mercutio and Tybalt sit back to back on stools.   On a given command they strike at each other.   Mercutio cheats by turning to face Tybalt without him knowing and scores several points.   Tybalt realizes he is being made a fool of and loses his temper.

1988

ROMEO AND JULIET

Director	**Les Waters**
Romeo	**Peter MacNichol**
Juliet	**Cynthia Nixon**

Mercutio	*Courtney Vance*
Tybalt	*Rob Knepper*
Nurse	*Anne Meara*
PARIS	*Bradley Whitford*

This time we decided to make Mercutio very playful and crafty. Tybalt enters and Mercutio sets him up. Mercutio is not being taken seriously by Tybalt. In comes Romeo. Tybalt goads Romeo and finally spits at him, Romeo takes it, Mercutio goes crazy. All lose respect for Romeo. As Tybalt and his cronies start to exit Mercutio sets up a game that Tybalt recognizes, "You rat catcher will you walk" and holds up a blindfold. The game is this-both combatants are blindfolded and the object is to try to hit the other guy, best of three. Tybalt has just had one victory over Romeo by humiliating him and now he is going to teach Mercutio a lesson. They are both blindfolded, Mercutio's guys creep up behind Tybalt's guys and hold knives to their throats so they can't warn Tybalt. Benvolio takes off Mercutio's blindfold and now the fun begins. You can imagine a sighted Mercutio leading blindfolded Tybalt into some pretty wonderful moves. When they cannot stand the prank any more they all crack up and Tybalt is made to feel a complete fool. He goes crazy and as in the normal version he kills Mercutio under Romeo's arm. Needless to say when we showed Joe Papp he hated the whole idea and eventually after a long fight between him and the director Les Waters, we had to cut it, but those who saw it had a great time. Well, that's the way it goes! Making up a game with the actors can enhance their characters and add another insight into the human condition.

It sets into motion a game gone wrong, a bunch of kids out of control.

I try to use the other boys to create a sense of chaos.

Chapter 18

Here are some simple crowd tricks.

1. As an exercise, place an actor with a sword in the center of the crowd. As he swings and cuts with the sword the crowd reacts as if the blade were about to come loose from the hilt. The crowd should avoid the point and the blade at all times. With this information the crowd will all duck, as the point travels over their heads, and jump to one side or the other on a lunge, never ever being in line with the point.
2. As the fight moves the crowd travels with the fight keeping the same distance from the combatants.
3. Combine both.
4. The crowd should always be moving, flowing with the action.
5. When Romeo stands still, being the only one not in motion, he will draw attention to himself, which is what we want, and he can speak his lines.
6. The crowd should always be a separate audience from the real audience.
7. Clapping at a well executed piece of choreography is not good.

8. Applauding a character's escape from a dangerous moment is good.

9. Shouting. No shout should be understandable. "Stick it to him", "bash his head in" "kick him in the .....s" apart from sounding anachronistic, are just too much information. I have found that for generic shouting, one of the most successful tricks, is to use swear words, but remove all the consonants.

10. A crowd can, by turning collectively in one direction, throw focus onto a specific piece of action. The entrance of the Prince, for example.

Chapter 19

Rudolf Nureyev

1977

Romeo and Juliet

Ballet Version

Director	*Rudolf Nureyev*
Romeo	*Rudolf Nureyev*
Mercutio	*Nicholas Johnson*
Tybalt	*Rick Warner*

I quote from a Paris newspaper: *His quick-moving version stays close to Shakespeare's play which he read and reread incessantly. Convinced that Elizabethan England and Renaissance Verona were both highly sexual and violent times, as is the world today, he chose to emphasize the social conflict of the feuding families. He developed the characters of the spirited Mercutio, champion of the Montagues, and Tybalt, the dangerous, vindictive, Mafioso leader of the Capulets as well as the role of Paris which he created for the young Laurent Hilaire.*

The crowd scenes, the Capulet ball, and the electrifying swordfights are magnificent, and demonstrate one of Nureyev's main aims as director in Paris; to give as many opportunities to as many dancers as he could.

You will notice that I am not credited with the fight direction. Such is the world of ballet and Rudolf Nureyev.

Rudolf Nureyev was a pain in the "proverbial", brilliant, creative and totally useless when it came to the fights. Used to indicating through his body, it was hard for him to express objectivity through the sword. He always looked like a bad version of Douglas Fairbanks. He was, however, a brilliant choreographer and after spending three months with him I was never ever the same fight director again. He had an amazing ability to tell stories through movement and come up with the unexpected. One example-when Mercutio was run through, nobody on stage was witness to the blow. They were all looking in the other direction. The only two people who knew what happened were Mercutio and Tybalt. So when the crowd sees Tybalt run off they all think Mercutio has won. Mercutio goes into his death throes and all the crowd think he is pretending. They copy his dying moves, laughing and having a good time. We, the audience, are privy to the fatal blow, so all we can do is to wait for Mercutio to die and for Romeo to realize what has happened. Romeo goes from complete relief to total anger-what a journey for the human spirit. For me this study of the human condition is what I search for in all my fights. Rudolf taught me the value of a crowd as a way of adding yet another dimension to the fight.

1978

R & J for Director Nagle Jackson

Cast

Randy Mel	*Tybalt*
Tom Robbins	*Mercutio*
Dan Corcoran	*Benvolio*

I was in England when I got the call to do this R&J for The Acting Company. " Is there anything that is special about your Romeo and Juliet that I need to know?" I asked Nagle ."Yes", he replied. "I believe that the reason Mercutio is so bitter is that he is crippled."" Oh! ," I replied, "that is going to affect the fights." So I choreographed a complicated fight based on a crippled Mercutio. I was quite pleased with the outcome. The actor playing Mercutio was one of my ex students and was very adept. The stinger to this story-during the "techs" Nagle came to me and said " I think I have made a mistake about Mercutio being crippled, I want to cut the idea." I went home thinking evil thoughts about killing directors who could not make up their minds. The next day I re-choreographed and my solution was to wound Mercutio in the leg on the first pass.

The Bigger the problem better the answer!!!!!

Chapter 20

The final blow on Mercutio.

MERCUTIO

Why the devil came you between us?

I was hurt under your arm.

Following the text is a must at this moment, namely because I cannot think of a better way to blame Romeo and make Mercutio's death Romeo's fault..

TYBALT under ROMEO's arm stabs MERCUTIO, and flies

with his followers

MERCUTIO

I was hurt under your arm.

There are many ways to achieve this.

Romeo breaks free of Benvolio's grip, runs in to stop the fight, grabbing Mercutio's sword arm. Romeo grabs Tybalt, getting in the way of Mercutio's blow and Tybalt takes the advantage.

My favorite is to make the audience feel, just before the final stab, that Mercutio has won. Mercutio is celebrating and it looks as if the fight is all over. Tybalt launches himself at Mercutio, who cannot defend himself because Romeo has hold of him. The stage picture of Romeo with his back to Tybalt with Mercutio vainly trying defend himself and Tybalt's lunge penetrating his body is classic. Needless to say the focus should be on Mercutio's face.

MERCUTIO

True, I talk of dreams,

Which are the children of an idle brain,

Begot of nothing but vain fantasy.

Which is as thin of substance as the air,

And more inconstant than the wind,who woos

Even now the frozen bosom of the north,

And being anger'd puffs away from thence,

Turning his face to the dew dropping south.

Imagine Romeo holding onto and in front of the figure on the left.

I have even toyed with the idea that as Romeo steps in to stop the fight Tybalt lunges at Romeo. Seeing this, Mercutio spins him out of the out of the way and takes the blow himself No matter how you do it, essentially it has to be **Romeo's fault** that Mercutio got mortally wounded.

We should now move on to the Romeo fight.
Reenter BENVOLIO

BENVOLIO

O Romeo, Romeo, brave Mercutio's dead!

That gallant spirit hath aspired the clouds,

Which too untimely here did scorn the earth.

ROMEO

This day's black fate on more days doth depend;

This but begins the woe, others must end.

BENVOLIO

Here comes the furious Tybalt back again.

If you were to take this moment away from the play we would, besides not having the death of Tybalt, have a huge emotional hole that could only be resolved by a fight. Perhaps the first part of the fight was an accident, but the second part is predetermined.

Timothy Dalton and Bernard Lloyd

ROMEO

Alive, in triumph! and Mercutio slain!

Away to heaven, respective lenity,

And fire-eyed fury be my conduct now!

Reenter TYBALT

Now, Tybalt, take the villain back again,

That late thou gavest me; for Mercutio's soul

Is but a little way above our heads,

Staying for thine to keep him company:

Either thou, or I, or both, must go with him.

TYBALT

Thou, wretched boy, that didst consort him here,

Shalt with him hence.

ROMEO

This shall determine that.

They fight; TYBALT falls

BENVOLIO

Romeo, away, be gone!

The citizens are up, and Tybalt slain.

Stand not amazed: the prince will doom thee death,

If thou art taken: hence, be gone, away!

ROMEO

O, I am fortune's fool.

This is the line that I believe encapsulates the whole fight.

Fate! Fate!

At this moment I do not want to hear applause for the fight. We as an audience should feel the remorse that Romeo feels. Our emotions should be stretched to the max. The death of Tybalt seals the fate of Romeo and Juliet. For the audience the fun part of the story is finished. From this moment on our tale is going to end in tears.

It was in Nagle Jackson's' production that I used one blow to kill Tybalt.

ROMEO

This shall determine that.

Romeo ran at Tybalt knocked his sword out of his hand and plunged in the dagger, pushing it further in as they fell to the floor.

Chapter 21

The Romeo Tybalt fight.

W hy does Tybalt come back? Apart from " it says so in the script."

IF-

He is being chased by the guards,

He is coming back to finish off Romeo,

He left his sword behind.

All I can say is-it is now that he finds out that Mercutio is dead. I feel that the fighting is over and that all that is needed is the death of Tybalt.

Back to David Suchet's Tybalt with Timothy Dalton at Royal Shakespeare Festival. Romeo now learns that Mercutio is dead and that he now has no other recourse but to find Tybalt and kill him. At this moment as Romeo runs offstage, Benvolio sees Tybalt coming back and yells to Romeo (played by Timothy Dalton), to come back.

BENVOLIO

Here comes the furious Tybalt back again.

Fate, Oh Fate!.If Romeo had been out of earshot.... Tybalt learns from Romeo that he has killed Mercutio and at last has proved to himself that he can go through with a duel. With great glee Tybalt takes on Romeo. In this production, Tybalt leapt from a balcony onto the stage. This was the dangerous moment in the fight. I hate gravity and adrenaline, because they can cause the most accidents. Romeo doesn't care if this a fair fight. He only knows that he has to kill Tybalt. So the fight looks and feels completely different. Gone are the jokes and in their place are the moves of a man who will kill or be killed. The sword is finally knocked out Tybalt's hand and Romeo sends Tybalt flying upstage into a corner of the set. Romeo advances, cornering Tybalt, and with his dagger stabs Tybalt repeatedly. Both Tybalt and Romeo are screaming as they do this. The crowd drags a demented Romeo off Tybalt. Tybalt lies dying at Romeo's feet. *"I am fortune's fool"*, cries Romeo- and we should be able to see that he was.

There are so many choices to be made here. What I used in the Royal Shakespeare's production was based on expediency. I choreographed a Long Mercutio fight, longer than usual, lot of acting, and a short Tybalt Romeo fight because of Timothy Dalton's limited rehearsal availability.

Now what happens when we take the fight away from Romeo?

He does not get a chance to show his love for Mercutio.

He does not get a chance to show that he really can take care of himself.

From a fight director's point of view, a Romeo who can stage fight really well could be a reason to extend the R v T fight and shorten the M v T fight if the Mercutio can't move. The values remain the same.

Chapter 22

Paris V. Romeo.

Finally we come to the Paris v Romeo fight. I believe this is one of the most brilliant fights scenes that Shakespeare ever invented. Take this scene away and what would be missing is a wonderful theatrical device called audience manipulation. If the scene were not there it would not be missed. Romeo would break into the tomb, find Juliet, and, thinking her dead, drink the poison. This is what he does anyway. Let Paris live.

What is clever about this fight is that, if we are paying attention, we want our hero to lose this fight. If Paris can delay Romeo or capture him, it will give Juliet a chance to wake up so that Romeo will find out that she is still alive.

Describing this fight as a delaying tactic gives us a wonderful chance to learn something about Paris and some more about Romeo's condition. Romeo comes to the tomb knowing he is going to die but needing to see Juliet before he kills himself.

Opens the tomb

From the dialogue we have a clear indication of what is going on.

PARIS

This is that banish'd haughty Montague,

That murder'd my love's cousin, with which grief,

It is supposed, the fair creature died;

And here is come to do some villanous shame

To the dead bodies: I will apprehend him.

Comes forward

He confronts Romeo with or without sword drawn. Either choice would say something about his character.

Sword Sheathed . I am in charge and am far superior to you and you will give up.

Sword drawn. I am wary of you and I am going to take charge by force.

PARIS

Stop thy unhallow'd toil, vile Montague!

Can vengeance be pursued further than death?

Condemned villain, I do apprehend thee:

Obey, and go with me; for thou must die.

Romeo tries to warn Paris not to go any further.

ROMEO

I must indeed; and therefore came I hither.

Good gentle youth, tempt not a desperate man;

Fly hence, and leave me: think upon these gone;

Let them affright thee. I beseech thee, youth,

Put not another sin upon my head,

By urging me to fury: O, be gone!

By heaven, I love thee better than myself;

If this were a film I would do a shot of Juliet stirring. This would remind us that she is not dead and is about to gain consciousness, if only Romeo could be delayed a little longer.

For I come hither arm'd against myself:

Stay not, be gone; live, and hereafter say,

A madman's mercy bade thee run away.

PARIS

I do defy thy conjurations,

And apprehend thee for a felon here.

ROMEO

Wilt thou provoke me? then have at thee, boy!

They fight

I seem to always come up with the same solution for the action, or variations on this theme.

Romeo attacks. I believe that he is not out to kill, only to render his assailant unconscious. Remember he doesn't know it is Paris whom he is fighting.

Note to lighting designer, not too dark please. Theatrical licence, we can pretend it's really dark.

A) Thanks

ROMEO

In faith, I will. Let me peruse this face. Mercutio's kinsman,

noble County Paris!

B) Paris looks as if he is going to win.
C) Romeo knocks him out.

Romeo goes back to the gates, opens them. A revived Paris runs at him and Romeo either by accident or design mortally wounds Paris. This moment could be more brutal but I feel that the time has come to let fate take its course. There is no way back for Romeo. He has killed yet again and even if Juliet were to wake up, Romeo is up the creek without a paddle by killing Paris.

PARIS

O, I am slain!

Falls

If thou be merciful,

Open the tomb, lay me with Juliet.

Dies

Side note; **O, give me thy hand** .

Use this line to have Paris help himself into the grave with Romeo's help, rather than Romeo having to drag him. It causes less wear and tear on the costumes and enables Romeo to show some compassion for Paris.

Chapter 23

All that is left is Juliet's death.

W *hat a great scene.*
She wakes and discovers Friar Laurence.
All must be well.
She finds out that Romeo is dead.
O. M. G.
Friar offers her an escape, she refuses.

He leaves.
She tries to poison herself, there is no poison left.
All the time the watch is getting nearer.

In any great action moment there is a "ticking clock" a dilemma made more urgent by an outside influence. In this case, it is discovery. The watch getting nearer is a great ticking clock. No pun intended. What do we the audience want?

Do we want to kill herself and be with Romeo?

If you are a father of a girl, as I am, you would want her to live.

Either way we will feel the same. Helpless as the play nears its end.

It says in the script that Juliet snatches the dagger, the word snatches, suggests fast. She is about to be discovered by the watch.

JULIET

Yea, noise? then I'll be brief. O happy dagger!

Snatching ROMEO's dagger

This is thy sheath;

Stabs herself

there rust, and let me die.

Falls on ROMEO's body, and dies.
There are two ways to approach this moment.
1 Put the audience ahead.

She pulls out dagger raises it, says the line, then stabs herself.

Juliet takes the dagger places it below her rib cage in full view of the audience, says the lines, turns upstage and out of sight of the audience plunges in the dagger.

Or
2 Put the audience behind.

She stabs herself and then says the line.

Takes the dagger turns upstage stabs herself and turns to the audience with the dagger sticking out of her.

In the ballet and in the opera Juliet wakes up just after Romeo has taken the poison and the two of them head for the door and Romeo collapses and dies. She follows.

Not happy with three deaths Shakespeare adds a fourth.

MONTAGUE

Alas, my liege, my wife is dead to-night;

Grief of my son's exile hath stopp'd her breath:

What further woe conspires against mine age?

And so ends this tragic tale.
The only danger left is for the Prince. His last lines are;

PRINCE

For never was a story of more woe

Than this of Juliet and her Romeo.

And not

For never was a story of more woe

Than this of Romeo and his Julio......

Chapter 24

Summation list.

W hen you meet the Director ask

What is your concept, vision?

In what period is the play set?

What would you feel is missing if the fight were not in the play?

Do you want to use blood?

Anything else I need to know?

How much time have you allocated for rehearsal?

COSTUMES

Can the actor move easily in the costume?

Are there going to be hats?

How are the swords going to be worn?

What type of sword hilt colors, brass, steel,gun metal?

(Shoe soles. Non Slip.

Shirts ,look out for loose ribbons!)

SET

How much space is there going to be?

Is the stage raked?

What is the surface going to be like?
Are there steps or any other major stage pieces?

LIGHTS

Keep above 45 degrees.

THE ACTORS

What would be missing from your character if the fight were to be removed from the play?

Do you have any special requests?

Do you have any physical limitations?

What you like to see in this fight?

Chapter 25

Generic 1st Fight.

S ampson pushes Gregory forward he bumps into Abraham who has is back to Gregory

SAMPSON

Remember thy washing blow.

Throws quarter staff to Gregory.
Abraham explodes into violence driving Gregory back by raining blows at him.
Gregory runs for his life.

Abraham turns on Sampson who is weaponless.
Sampson manages to grab Abraham's staff.
They struggle Sampson gets staff.
Serving man grabs staff from Sampson.
Gregory returns to the fray swings at servingman who ducks and Sampson takes the blow.
They are about to come together again when in between them steps....

BENVOLIO

Part, fools!

Put up your swords[staves]; you know not what you do.

Beats down their swords, staves.
In steps...   **Tybalt** Stage Left.

TYBALT

What, art thou drawn among these heartless hinds?

Tybalt's boys,Sampson and Gregory, who are on Stage Right
run to Tybalt and stand behind him.

Turn thee, Benvolio, look upon thy death.

Benvolio takes his two guys and is about to leave stage right.

BENVOLIO

I do but keep the peace: put up thy sword,

Or manage it to part these men with me.

He goes, pushing servants before him.

TYBALT

What, drawn, and talk of peace! I hate the word,

As I hate hell, all Montagues, and thee:

Benvolio continues to leave.

Have at thee, coward!

Tybalt's guys laugh. Benvolio turns to his two servants who
look to see what he will do. Benvolio has to fight
They fight

Tybalt easily beats Benvolio's first attack.

In doing so he causes Benvolio to crash into other tradespeople which sets off a chain reaction.

Crowd fight.

This should involve any market objects such as brooms, trays, vegetables, etc.

You might have the crowd tip over a cart.

Tybalt drives Benvolio off, followed by the servants cheering.

Enter, several of both houses, who join the fray; then enter Citizens, with clubs.

FIRST CITIZEN

Clubs, bills, and partisans! strike! beat them down!

Down with the Capulets! down with the Montagues!

Enter CAPULET in his gown, and LADY CAPULET

CAPULET

What noise is this? Give me my long sword, ho!

LADY CAPULET

A crutch, a crutch! why call you for a sword?

CAPULET

My sword, I say! Old Montague is come,

And flourishes his blade in spite of me.

Enter MONTAGUE and LADY MONTAGUE

MONTAGUE

Thou villain Capulet,--Hold me not, let me go.

LADY MONTAGUE

Thou shalt not stir a foot to seek a foe.

Montague throws the wife off and attacks Capulet. Fight with Long Swords {one Pass}
  Enter PRINCE, with Attendants

PRINCE

Rebellious subjects, enemies to peace,

Profaners of this neighbour-stained steel,

Will they not hear? What, ho! You men, you beasts,

That quench the fire of your pernicious rage

With purple fountains issuing from your veins,

On pain of torture, from those bloody hands

Throw your mistemper'd weapons to the ground,

And hear the sentence of your moved prince.

Everybody stops fighting.   Enter Tybalt chased by Benvolio. Tybalt makes it look as if Benvolio is the aggressor. The Prince takes the sword out of Benvolio's hand. Benvolio drops to the floor.

Three civil brawls, bred of an airy word,

By thee, old Capulet, and Montague,

Have thrice disturb'd the quiet of our streets,

And made Verona's ancient citizens

Cast by their grave beseeming ornaments,

To wield old partisans, in hands as old,

Canker'd with peace, to part your canker'd hate:

If ever you disturb our streets again,

Your lives shall pay the forfeit of the peace.

Once more, on pain of death, all men depart.

This is only an indication of how the first fight might take place. Tell a good story, illuminate the text and the characters with action and above all...... **BE SAFE.**

Chapter 26

The certificate of proficiency in stage fighting.

In a meeting of The Society Of British Fight Directors we decided to award a certificate of proficiency for stage fighting. The idea was to give our students proof that they had had some training in stage combat. We divised a test which was made up of creating a scene that included choreography that had been set by the combat teacher at each Drama School. Bill Hobbs and myself suggested an upgrade to the test to give special merit to talented fighters. Not all students passed and a limited number received the upgrade. The first test of this sort in America was at Carnegie Mellon University in the early seventies where I was teaching and it was presided over by Paddy Crean.

Fight Warm up

Although it was standard practice for actors in England to go through the fights before the show, when I first came to the USA this was not the norm. My students Randy Kovitz and Nels Hennum worked hard and long collecting signatures to support the idea of using Fight Captains and doing Fight warm ups. We were backed by American Equity but it was those two men who did all the hard work. Fight Captains and doing fight warm ups are now standard in the theater but without their dedication we probably would have had a lot more accidents here in the USA.

The fight warm up should consist of running through all the fights slowly to iron out any problems that may have occurred during the previous night's performance. The wrongly delivered blow, the excessively enthusiastic grab and many other adjustments if left uncorrected could lead to an injury. Verbal interaction should be encouraged so that the errors in a fight can be sorted out and corrected. The fight captain is an advocate for the actors and it is he or she who is responsible for the fights.

Choose your fight captain carefully.

The job description-Someone who can be calm in a crisis. Someone who can help correct the errors of the previous performance, and maintain the choreography. There have been cases when an adjustment needs to take place in the action sequences due to an added prop or some other unforeseen problem. If this is the case, he or she should contact the fight director and ask his advice on what to do. Being the fight captain does not give permission to change the fight after the fight director has gone as happens in some cases. If the fight director knows his job his choreography will hold up under the pressure of performance and will not need changing.

Good luck with your fights and try not to......... **BREAK A LEG.**